D0617077

TICKER

TICKER

Mark Neely

LOST HORSE PRESS
Sandpoint, Idaho

Printed in America.
All Rights Reserved.

No part of this book may be reproduced or transmitted in any form or by any means, electronic or mechanical, including photocopy, recording, or any information storage and retrieval system now known or to be invented, without permission in writing from the publisher, except by a reviewer who wishes to quote brief passages in connection with a review written for inclusion in a magazine, newspaper, or broadcast.

Copyright © 2021 by Mark Neely.

Cover Painting: Untitled /Zonder titel, 2005, Oil on toned gelatin silver print, 49.5 x 65.5" (127 x 168 cm), ©Teun Hocks, courtesy Torch Gallery, Amsterdam, Netherlands; Paci Contemporary, Brescia, Italy; Fahey/Klein Gallery, Los Angeles, USA.
Author Photo: Jill Christman.
Book Design: Christine Lysnewycz Holbert.

FIRST EDITION

This and other fine LOST HORSE PRESS titles may be viewed on our website at www.losthorsepress.org.

LIBRARY OF CONGRESS CATALOGING-IN-PUBLICATION DATA

Cataloging-in-Publication Data may be obtained from the Library of Congress.
ISBN 978-1-7333400-9-0

for Ella and Henry

CONTENTS

I

Blood Type

II

Interior Survey

III *Sent Us of the Air*

IV *Supernova*

I
BLOOD TYPE

SUBVOCAL (CHALLENGER)

Age of *Achille Lauro* and *Rainbow Warrior*,
of *Mad Max* and the doddering Gipper,

of plaid-clad women and mustachioed men
tossing villains through plate glass. Of Jan Hammer,

Desperately Seeking Susan, "Easy Lover,"
of Gorbechev with his skull cracked open.

Age of Sweetness and the Refrigerator.
Age of *I love it when a plan comes together.*

And the jittery schoolroom television where I watched
the launch become a strange white praying

mantis in the sky. *Obviously a major malfunction.*
It was happiness, taunting the three-fingered girl

who moused along the playground fence.
It was life when her brothers, thick-tongued

and rough as the broken sidewalk,
came hulking from an alley

to kick my skinny ribs in. The bruising was
an unexpected pleasure. I must have dreamed

the rocket boosters corkscrewing away.
Who could have known

days later I'd be smoking Winstons
in an abandoned mansion as girls stepped

through windows in Brooke Shields jeans,
dust floating in the sunlight

like our nebulous desires. Who could have imagined
all the stupid years to come, the wreckage

falling toward the ocean—
surface of the suffocating dark.

AUTOMATON

There goes another mountainside
of trees, mown down by orange rovers
and burned to fuel Bruce's mouth—an engine
designed to run forever, like Edison's fabled bulb,
like Takeru Kobayashi
who downed fifty-seven cow brains once.
When Bruce eats a hamburger he can't stop
picturing the bolt pistol, the French
on the other hand fork up *blanquette de veau*
while lovingly remembering the birth. The Hadron Collider
whirls beneath their houses, simulating the vast forces
between Bruce's ears. The Amish won't go near it.
They believe modern machines
are the devil's work—probably right. They believe
we're spinning on a wheel of stars
designed to separate the living from the dead
like an Iranian centrifuge. In the future
only the Amish will be famous. The rest of us
will live happily underground, protected from falling
satellites and the nuclear sky. The sun's sick
furnace roars, agitating every molecule
of Bruce's body. He spreads his gauzy lungs
like wet wings.

OOF

A flurry of marriages, births. Then pause—
the generation
wringing itself out. Welcome to the long
trough of middle age, where our hero flinches

as he bends to tie his shoe.
Annie says you know you're getting old
if you pull yourself from the car
with an involuntary *oof.*

Bruce makes such noises all the livelong day,
an orchestra of grunts and rumbles
led by a sadist with a bent baton.
He looks wrong, smells wrong—

his various crannies acrid as mythical swamps.
There must be a cereal or miracle
fruit somewhere . . . But what have we here?
A tattooed, crimson-lipped checker

hidden among the usual pensioners, weighing pears
between blue fingernails. Bruce veers
into her aisle. She rings him through,
zipping veggies and vitamins across the scanner beam

with the cheerful efficiency of the young.
Have a nice day, she says, then catches
his delinquent glance and adds a cruel, *Sir,*
and a pitiless smirk. Poor Bruce,

he isn't sure what happened.
Gone from suitor to lecher in a wink.
And really, he's no dirtier than before.
Just old. Just older.

FIRST BLOOD

Starting with Rambo he wanted a knife, starting
with cub scouts and scuffed plastic soldiers half-
buried in mud, starting behind Holy Cross where his friend
slit Bruce's finger and smeared their bloody
hands together, where the neighbor girl
lifted her shirt. She was older, braver. *Show us your boobs*,

the friend said, and there was her pale, freckled chest.
Starting with race we divide into clans, starting
with gifted and slow, muscled and gawky, girls
and boys, starting with money, the haves
and have-nots, princesses and paupers, starting with blood
kin and strangers, so not even Jesus can friend

everyone, so no one has six billion followers. Bruce's friend
is a cop in Chicago and does that cop thing with his chest.
He tweets *#AllLivesMatter*. Not even the blood
of martyrs can satisfy everyone. Starting with status. Starting
with skin. The cop is biracial, a hyphen-American, half
someone, half someone else. The girl

grew up. She lives in Fort Lauderdale with girls
of her own. She works for the Navy, not much of a friend
anymore except on Facebook, nowhere. *We all have
our flaws*, say the prophets, the movies, the breasts
in the mirror. But this cop is being a prick. He's starting
to tick everyone off. In *First Blood*'s

opening scene, there's no hint of the bloodletting
to come, only a decrepit outbuilding, boys playing, a girl
and her mother stringing clothes on a line. The shot starts
with Stallone in the distance, unrecognizable, neither friend

nor enemy yet. *Excuse me,* he says, from deep in his chest.
The film's first words. So soft you could easily miss them. He has

almost nothing, a sleeping bag slung on his shoulder, has
the knife of course, but tucked away, bloody
no more. And a flag on his chest
from the war. The mother shoos the girl
in the house when Rambo asks after his friend,
who it turns out was dead from the start.

Begin with the knife, the girl he can't have,
the four types of blood: family, friendship,
period, lung. Start with a hole in his chest.

SUBVOCAL (CAPITAL)

The easy shape of mama's nipple, red
hair falling in yr sticky face. Packets of chalky

chocolate mixed thinly with warm water,
tee shirt drying on the radiator,

screen door not quite
flush. Dew tells

you the time. And a penny for each rewinding
of "Papa Don't Preach" on the VHS,

each hopeful peek
at the neighbor girl's drawn blinds. Now

yr regressing, tossing rocks
through the nutso neighbor's window,

shoplifting *Penthouse* and Skoal,
puking on the White House lawn.

Putting it all down in a crooked hand.
No wonder yr face

feels like a U-Haul
packed with fertilizer.

Because Dad never took you fishing.
Because the President didn't take

yr death threats serious. Oh how you miss
the sweet smoke of a Marlboro

under yr wings. Because with each grief
you care less. Yr therapist frowns.

Yr father's either a cartoon demon peeling away
in a flurry of curses and exhaust,

or he's just a hapless ghost.
You won't get any sympathy for that.

And here comes Mother
flying in with a brick

in one hand, a feather in the other.
It's funny,

those days melt into the smallest coins.
They jingle in yr pocket.

CURRICULUM

Remember how we won the West
by dressing the horses in women's clothes
and ferrying a herd of elephants
across the Rhone. How Bruce
snuck into Annie's room, unspooling
a length of orange thread, how they clung
to the fallen hero's body,
were dragged aboard the flaming ships
and sailed away. How riotous
we were when Bruce
refused the crown. How
we crowded around the radio
while he spun tales of childhood
folly, and all the women
wore the dresses Annie wore,
and the White House was a sort of palace,
Bruce strolling pensive and helmetless
on the perfect lawn. Remember Annie
crawling over the back seat, trying
to put him back together. How he slumped
inside the horse, breathing the hot stink
of a soldier's breath, while our enemies
did the rough work, cursing, shouting
orders, of dragging the giant creature
through the breach. How Bruce leapt
from a secret door, tore
off his moldering clothes
and began his famous speech
as the sun drove its cattle
over the ruined wall
and Annie lay in a dusty tent,
dreaming of Paris's special talent.

TWO DIMENSIONS

once he was a soldier   he swung his shovel
and excavated underground palaces   kicked up a choking dust
for the President   he cleaned his rifle
thinking back   every evening
to the night crawlers he used to catch   crouched like a frog
passing a light over their banded bodies   in the grass
as they sunned themselves   the village was subsumed
in darkness   he'd wake up early   he could barely see
and cast into the lake   the blue temple
where bass were always waiting   beyond the cypress grove
when each day was a door   he walked through once

DRONE VIEW

Take a dyslexic Lego set . . . a ripped edition
of *The Ego and the Id* . . . a TV graveyard
and the chintzy props
for a small town *Our Town*

and wire Bruce together . . . place
him on a hill overlooking the pleasant village
where he will be born . . . he stumbles
into being . . . no great threat

to the money men . . . a shadow
of the shadow government . . . hardly anyone
notices the glitch
in his gait . . . the tiny sparking

of his eyes . . . the days
he can't get out of bed . . . at night
swarms of mysterious birds
tear through the dark . . . their instructions

like a radio you barely hear . . . alone
in the buzzing living room
Bruce waits for orders . . . the ceiling
might as well be gauze . . .

like a teenager sending blue letters
overseas . . . he tells them
everything . . . the walls quiver
with pleasure . . . the house is

a hall of smashed mirrors . . .
he doesn't worry . . . the machines
will always care for us . . . they
will bury us.

REALITY TV

Bruce believes in everything—
even the fat Arkansan shoving his
pale hand in a river orifice
to pull an oily, boy-sized
catfish from the muck.
He understands the urge to tangle
with a horror-faced, primeval
beast and win, to suffer
the slice of a fin or bar
brawl fist, terrified of feeling
nothing. He even believes
in democracy, though it's clear
we're all a bunch of frightened
worms, burrowing blind and hungry
through the precarious earth.
On another channel, men live
in the wild and grow ridiculous
beards—one checks a deadfall trap
and carries the rabbit home
by its lucky feet, its upside-down
ears pricked, listening for whatever
comes after the tunneling.
It's all too much for Bruce.
He's embarrassed by his pantry
full of pasta and canned fish.
No one can see you Bruce,
says the voice inside his head.

SUBVOCAL (HONKY)

From a motorcade speeding through Dallas,
from the frigid body

of a Boeing jet, from semis
stuffed with rotting lettuce, train cars

lugging tons of oil and grain, from icy skyscrapers
and wooded haunts, from Mr. Potato Head and Honest Abe,

Jefferson and Bloody Mary, from a Silverado's
headlights in the campfire, or the *logos*

of a sensible sedan, I spring,
blow steam and down

another burned coffee, the beans
gone to the moon

and back for my displeasure. I traverse
a snowy pass, wave my motley flag, spying

down the barrel of grandfather's gun —
like Chekhov, like Dirty Harry, like

Dick Cheney. I bring a flung duck down
and strut and strut, calling for a bible

and a box of bullets, calling for higher fences,
stricter sanctions, a new crackdown. Calling for

bulgogi, lamb vindaloo, Jamaican jerk,
for football Thursday nights, for concussion

protocols. I can roll a joint like nobody's business,
roll an SUV on Friday night

and be back at the desk by Monday, seven sharp,
singing shanties. I'm handy

with a chef's knife, Skilsaw, fly rod,
pipe bomb. I love the shock wave

of my body hitting Lake Decatur, sending fish
in all directions, sending them to their extinction.

I love private beaches, abstract art, alt porn,
uphill marathons. I like my politics

and my martinis dirty. I play golf badly.
I play golf with a Frisbee!

I'm a genius from the free throw line.
Once a week I slide around the queen

bed slick with love, juiced out of my skull,
half *Kama Sutra*, half Venn diagram.

I score some Molly, Bennies, Oxy, some sick *mota*.
I shred the documents like Bill and Hillary,

like Ollie North and Fawn Hall.
I can work the hell out of a pair of khakis.

I deny it all. For the smog settling in the valley,
for the gutted grocery

and crumbling jetty, for the three pages in the dictionary
that begin with *death-*, I am responsible.

Honky, lost container ship, gull-spill,
bleached flower. I crowd you from the armrest,

from the voting booth, from the shaky frame.
I throw Old Glory over yr coffin, throw

money on the bed, throw yr ass in jail.
My rifling allows me

to fly one thousand miles
an hour through the planet's heart.

My night terrors make me wonder
what Daddy did to me. My murders barely

make the papers. Not so long ago
I gunked out of the muck,

peat bog, slag heap, strip mine, stinking
holler, reeking of creosote, paper pulp,

night sweat and corn oil, reeking
of sulfur and history.

I limped over a burned hillside, eyeing
a village in the valley.

I needed to wash it off.
I needed to wash it off of everyone.

II INTERIOR SURVEY

HOMUNCULUS

Sunlight pours into the Russian theater
of Bruce's brain. His one eye skims
each gaudy costume like a humming-
bird cracked-out on blooms.
The music stops. Rusted antlers
twist from his skull and tangle in a truss
of lights as he jigs across the deck
in concrete shoes, wondering where
to put his concrete cock. His heart spills
over like a vat of pulp. Pining for a lover,
he sees his own face in the wavering water—
a system of fleshy vents shuttles cold air in,
warm out. Through these intricate channels
seeps the secret police's poison gas.

SUBVOCAL (SUPERMODEL)

I go slowly crazy in this graceless cage,
a stadium singer

stuck in the trappings of a middle manager,
a spirit meant to sin, press palms, stalk the cat-

walk with a crew of gorgeous acolytes.
Instead I peer through the bars of Bruce's eyes,

biding time in the middle of the Middle West,
where raking leaves is conversation, where dying

is an occupation. Each day we pass
the same decrepit CVS, same

stone-faced Catholic church,
same Doberman lunging

at its fence. Each night I pray for some séance
or surgery to cleave me

from this married body, this scribbled grocery list
Bruce calls a brain.

Let me leap up dancing on the table!
Let me screw my way through South America

like the secret service. Let me take a bullet
for the President, feel the fast life rip through my skin.

Anything but this endless wintering.
Anything but another community theater *Peter Pan.*

We're heading home. Bruce Jr. babbles in his car seat.
His father gazes at the shadowy

maples lining the neighborhood—
fucking maples—

and proclaims these clichés *Beautiful.*
Even the kid knows he's a fool. Five thousand years

of history and that's what he comes up with?
Beautiful.

THE ECONOMY STUPID

Like a Taco Bell built
on the site of a desecrated
burial mound,

Bruce often forgets
to be despondent
over everything

we have burned,
bulldozed, hauled
away. His attention

is drawn to clean
lines, gaudy billboards,
the eclipsed moon

hidden in the silent
bell. Unwrapping
another paper shroud,

he eats one-handed,
driving from city
to swamp, leaving

a trail of oily
tears. Always hungry
for the new

outrage, he scans
the radio for another
jingle. It's so easy

being Bruce.
He's open late.
He lets anybody in.

INSURGENCY

Saigon Execution:
Murder of a Vietcong
by Saigon Police Chief, 1968

Bruce remembers fighting in the wars,
thinking, *the Buddha will forgive me,*
his revolver inches from the temple
of a captured officer in an absurd
plaid shirt. But it can't be.
All this happened before Bruce
was even born. If anything he
inherited the murdered man's
astonishment. Once, after an ambush,
he marched across an archaic bridge
holding his eyes in a fist while the village
burned. He donned both uniforms.
He held the gun to his own wild brain.

BLACK BALLOON

let us release one more balloon   emptied of media
  filled with Bruce's breath   as cardinals blaze in the bushes
   and watch it wobble carelessly   outside the hospital
    into the high noise   where Annie appears pale and shaking
     where angels take our measure   among the madmen
     and we begin to fall   having had the lifeless baby
      deflated   sterile   separated from her body
      hollowed of meaning   cast into the brilliant sky

UNITED CHURCH OF BRUCE

In the dream a French cathedral
vaults up in the storm like God's own
battleship. Bruce wakes to the Freudian
implications and the sickly haze
of Central Indiana, stands by
while the dog takes an agitated piss,
then drives to a glassy arena
where he mouths the words
to "Be Thou My Vision," steals
looks at the put-together divorcées,
washes his sins in Mocha Java.

The Reverend climbs a metal staircase
and begins. Ashes. Urns. Coins
from his father's pockets.
The coins over our eyes. Everyone
stands like Jesus has them by the shirt.
Sunlight reddens Mary's hair
as she stares down with her many
faces—sullen daughter, terrified
teenage bride, sedated mother
whose son has died.

TOTEM

Bruce takes
a swig then
passes the bottle

to the Bruce
below and then
again until the

whole column
starts to wobble,
each Bruce kicking

at the Bruce
supporting him
like, *What the*

fuck? If this
dance keeps up
Bruce thinks

he'll find the
real Bruce down
there, the brave

big-hearted Bruce
who will lead the rest
of them to victory,

the slick fox-
Bruce—patient,
cunning, ready to

lunge from the wood,
but Bruce knows it's
no use. There

are nothing but
desperate Bruces
all the way down.

SUBVOCAL (COUNTERTERROR)

Liive from the fucking wires! From waves of mutant grain
and roiling ice. Liive from the bull-baiting self-

hating radio! From jiving pig megaphones
and philanthropy's murderous houses,

from detention stadium where a hurricane spins
down the drain to the tune of a squad car's

mesmeric lights. Liive from the oily interior,
the death cars pulling away. Dear pigs protect us.

Save us from swarthy bomb makers and teenage flame
wars and the hormonal fury of lip ring and tongue,

from the AKs under their hoodies, the poor and unstable,
from gas lines undermining our houses.

Dear pigs we salute you. Dear POTUS rock us to sleep!
Go liive from the high-value target, from playgrounds of rubble

and rebar. POTUS protect us!
We voted you into our billowing dreams.

Fence off the borders. Fence off this sadness.
Go liive from the blowing away!

From the scrubbed decks of history,
where loving pig fathers swill their swine wine,

where precious pig children toss in their beds.
Liive from their gossiping brains!

From the shiny new century, from satellites pinging at Mars.
From rabid star mags and orange alerts, from bloody night clubs

and the tight cockpits of F-15s. Liive from the force
field of privilege. We'll make this new testament ours!

Follow the sirens, the exquisite weapons.
Turn to the camera. Dance in the epileptic light.

Throw yr hands in the air.
Throw yr damn hands in the air!

THE EYES IN HIS HEAD

It's so retro—
checking out the bodies
in the checkout line.

The workout queen
posed beside the latest
Cosmo, the slick-

skirted professional
unloading Lean Cuisine
and pinot noir

onto the weathered
conveyor. Bruce flushes
when she flirts

with the college boy
bagging her Greek yogurt.
He tries to ignore

the murmur muttering,
You could build a shelf,
line up yr Shakespeare,

yr Adrienne Rich.
Thank God he's not
a woman, passing

before these foggy
mirrors, carrying
a mattress on his back.

Bruce feels bad enough
already, overfed
and dreadful

like an early atom
bomb. Fat Man
losing his grip

as the bay doors open,
the city's edges sharpening
under his stare.

MOORINGS

x.

here's our hero racing over the avenues of Paris
Hilton's airbrushed thighs, rapt

by the bedside as she thrashes in the sheets,

overdosed and ventilated, signaling
with a few clasps of her twiggy hand.
It's practically Marxian, rubbing up against

that kind of money. But not even
the vortex of Manhattan

                      can hold

x.

Bruce long. His father falls again—
on the icy drive, through a shower door,

off another speeding

wagon. He calls the saintly nurses whores.
They shut him up
in a urinous room, give him scraps

of envelope on which he scribbles daily
grievances, cryptic snippets of philosophy.

                    He keeps his pain

x.

like a survival fire. The TV blares
in the dark, where poachers

labor to butcher an adult giraffe.

Bruce is jealous of everyone else's adventures.
Only illness and marriage
he thinks, are more monotonous

than war—just his brand of foolishness.
Soon he'll shrivel like his father to a rotten core.

Anyway, Paris Hilton's

x.

fifteen minutes already went up her gorgeous
orifices. Bruce reminds

himself the world's religions

are more than backdrop
for his masturbation sessions. There are cities
waiting to be conquered. French actresses

who haven't got their Oscars yet. He follows his bliss
into a greasy alley,

follows the blood

x.

trail to a hotel room hung
with photos of the sea,

which mock his limping journeys

from soccer field to grocery store.
Once he blasted his heart pangs
through a Marshall stack. Once he stood

on the thirteenth floor, peering at a message
stenciled on a bus below:

DON'T JUMP

x.

don't sit around waiting for the faked orgasm
to be over. It's time for another

Zeno leap into the future!

To be swept away by Hurricane Whatever.
If only the leaves could stay glossy green
through November. If only Dad would get a little

better. Then the jetties could hold the oceans
in their bony hands forever. Forever

and ever. Whatever.

DEPOSITION

Bruce's jittery associates
line up outside his office, dying
to bring him their breakdowns—inner illnesses
exotic as the blue
heron he saw this morning,
standing regally in the mouth
of a sewer pipe. He keeps his own

anxieties at bay with a regimen
of leafy greens, black tea
and gin. Every other day
he runs five miles to keep
from shouting at his sulking son,
or railing on the internet
about the ecological catastrophe
of consumerism. For lunch, he drives
through the Tillotson McDonald's
for another Quarter Pounder.

Idling in the park, Bruce watches
cruisers and solitary eaters quell
their hungers. A pony-tailed jogger.
Sex is always on his mind—he fears
in his case, the every seven seconds estimate
might be a little high. He imagines migrants
kneeling in the lettuce, the feedlot stench.
The sludgy river oozes south. A giant harvester
sweeps Idaho to dust. Pursing his lips
around a last swallow of Diet Coke, Bruce
rests his head on the sun-warm window, the taste
of oil and advertising on his tongue.

SUBVOCAL (HADLEY)

Watch out for the failures,
the middle managers laughed out of art

school, sitting sulky and cross-legged
under the trees

of their ambition. It has to go somewhere,
like storm runoff washes over pesticidal

fields to find a river. Neither
Manson nor Hinckley could write a hook

to save their lives or we would have a few
more Californians and Reagan wouldn't be

such a boring hero. They say everyone
wants to be an artist. Not me.

I want to be debonair.
I want to rise on a throne of fire

and lash the cities with my seven arms,
so even the rich will have to pay attention.

Seung-Hui Cho
signed his stories with a question mark.

He wanted to be Jesus
and burn down the school where we learn

all this crap. Once, Hadley left a suitcase
of Hemingway's manuscripts on a train.

Now there's a story. Just thinking about it makes me nervous,
like watching video of the Dalai Lama brushing away

a huge mandala of colored sand, pouring it back
into nonexistence. Too bad we can't all be so cavalier.

Cho had locks, chains, hollow
points made to bloom in the brain

of Liviu Librescu who survived the Focşani ghetto
so he could die bracing a door.

Better scope out the exits. Better sit with your back
against a wall. Keep an eye on the nervous types, silent types,

guys in bulky jackets. Better check beneath your seat
for a suitcase full of stories, a backpack full of nails.

Better bow down to the body.

III

SENT US OF THE AIR

BRUCE IN THE CITY

Sidestepping warning signs
for falling icicles, Bruce
tips back his head
as oblivious shoppers
funnel down glittering
dirty Michigan Ave.,
beside the lake
of his recurring
dream. He coughs
in his sleeve, pops a few
pills, gives thanks
to pharmaceuticals
for keeping him
upright another day.

All the windows
he can't afford
have kindly clouded
over. Beyond rows
of glib citadels,
the lake heaves
like a philosophical
question, too vast
for ice. European
tourists cruise by
in oily coats.

Money-drugged,
he drags his aching
head through the
arid air, looking
for something

to make him feel
better. He steps
through a door
and the murmur
blares in his ears,
echoing the bedazzling
crowd, telling him
what he is worth.

MUSEUM OF NATURAL HISTORY

pale versions of them danced
  inside a diorama of Lakota hunters
   dim terraria where giant
    cockroaches clung in the corners
     Bruce Jr. crawled
      inside a blue whale's heart   tired
       they drank chalky milkshakes
        hunched over a greasy table
         surrounded by sullen teenagers
         talking

five minutes
  as significant as any
   prehistoric era
    Bruce stood
     over the body
      of the two-thousand year-old boy
       and read how embalmers
        scrambled the brain with a hook
         listening to the *ahh-huh-huhh*
         of their own breath

UNBORN ELEGY

On the gray shelf of winter,
in the dusty light
of 2:00 a.m., Bruce

sees his lost boy's face,
still imagining the dead
rising like balloons, though

by second grade he knew
in this universe
there's no such thing as up—

only a scattering
of matter speeding away
from a giant

bomb. It's strange
how Bruce misses him,
this boy he's never met

except as a kick
in Annie's belly, this
biohazard bag thrown

out with the bloody
needles, this notion falling
through him like a stone.

BRUCE'S FAITH

The secret is to be looking forward
to something beyond Friday night—
the Sunday long run or sitting
in a pew to pray away
two thousand bloody years.
Bruce dozes among the sinners,
imagining the fun he might have had
with Sally Wen if he hadn't been
such a mouse. He blames
the hymn for filling his head
with rapture, blames the minister
who mounts the stage, his hair
in shambles, like Kurt Cobain's
might look if he had been allowed to age.
A glowing teenager joins him
at the pulpit. She wants
them all to *like* the church
on Facebook. She uses Twitter
as a metaphor for prayer.
Bruce watches bird shadows pan
across stained glass, still
one piece of evidence away.

INTELLIGENT DESIGN

He thinks he made the universe
somehow—scattered stars,
decided if the trees
would leaf or needle,
dressed the beetle
in medieval armor.

It's not out of the question.
After he burned a moon-sized hole
in the ozone, razed the Amazon,
turned the endless plains
into a pile of bison skulls.

It took seven days.
It took seven billion years.
It takes all his breath
to keep this damn coal
smoldering.

So he doesn't get worked up
about another shooting.
From this dis-
tance even the bombings
bloom and die away.

It isn't even lonely.

OR LESS

Even Bruce has murderous thoughts
when he spots her latest lover's glossy
Lexus in his ex's driveway, or seethes
with eleven carefully counted items
while a clueless geezer unloads
a brimming cart, then pulls a moldering
checkbook from his pocket. A better
Bruce would reserve these furies
for the idiots holed up in congress,
for killer cops and planet-melting
CEOs, but the black conveyor's endless
spooling too closely mimics
his plodding brain, which blows
another gasket when the ex in question
parts the automatic doors,
some new Apollo on her heels.

STAR VEHICLE

He suspects the teenage lawyers
jaywalking to lunch in skinny suits,
the punk girl breaking down
boxes behind Vera Mae's,
the realtor sipping coffee in pink
power heels, and the beautiful hippie,
a mess of dreadlocks under his cap,
are all employees of a syndicate
whose mission is to lure him
to the cliff edge of sanity
and give a gentle push.

Listen to the sirens
like coyotes in the distance,
note the sky painted between buildings,
diffuse and limitless, suggesting
wanderlust.

Bruce is looking for the right bank job,
the scruffy orphan who brings his own youth
rushing back, the oddball teller
who can crack the dull force field
around his heart, the alien
disguised as one of us.

FAMOUS BRUCE

had his face plastered on every bus, his voice
piped through the multiplex, his name keyed hourly
into Google by a band of eager interns . . .

He was afraid no one would remember
the furious engine of his desire, afraid absence
would not make the heart

grow fonder at the implausible distances
of the afterlife. He tried it all:
mud baths, Kawasakis, convalescence,

even stealing off to coastal islands
with the governess. But on each new
window sill roosted the future's

patient pigeons,
cooing gently, calling him
back to insignificance.

SUBVOCAL (JEFFERSON AIRPLANE)

Yr a slut Bruce trapped in a cut-
rate popemobile, one step

behind the dweebs who went to Woodstock
for the music. Yr fantasies barely fill a Post-it,

yr rutting lands
in the rut of what you think

she wants. Bust out Bruce! Let's ditch
this midwest mopery

and belly up under a wall of antlers, or spar
with toned brokers in Brooklyn gyms.

Grunt. Steam. Maybe for once go home
with him. Whatever floats yr buoy Bruce!

Whatever revs that rusty apparatus
in yr chest. Kayak the Colorado!

Hike Slickrock Creek. Slosh
out two martinis and press yr mouth

to Annie's neck, just promise me
no more rolling to the middle

of the queen-size, neither of you
managing a sweat. We're not mowing

a lawn here Bruce! We're not
wiping a countertop and wringing

out the sponge. We're talking
Kumamotos and Cristal under a disco

swirl of stars, talking muddy hippies
wading Filippini Pond as Grace Slick wails.

Let's get going Bruce! Let's get
Catullan, Cassanovian, Kennedy-esque.

Make those fuckers wish
they still had bodies. It's time

to blow this awful subcommittee and take
a few more dizzy spins around the sun

before yr staring through six feet of Illinois,
an inch of cake makeup on yr face.

Are you listening? Bruce,
are you awake?

ICARUS AGAIN

He didn't like the way the obstetrician
flinched when he broke Annie's water,
or winked through her worst contractions
as if the two of them were watching
a campy horror film together. Nor
did he find the silver cross
nestled in the doc's chest hair
reassuring. They kept their distance
as the heat and noise
of Annie's terrible new power
filled the room. *This will be the end of you,*
said the murmur,
and a blue-robed coven
ringed the ruddy animal
and fed a tiny tube into her nose.
When she howled Bruce wasn't sure
whose throat the scream was coming from.
It was the end of him.

VIEW FROM THE HIGHWIRE

Saga in ticker tape,
with no occasion
for parading, Bruce's

stock is taking
a dive, his shares
brought low

by the brutality
of airline security,
secret prisons,

border agents
spewing black dust
from their white

Humvees, a TV
blaring, *May you live
in interesting times.*

See boyish Bruce
perched in the perfect
maple, cool

girls in tight red
gym shorts
passing below.

See *Hustler*
and furtive smokes
behind Holy Cross—

it seemed damned
interesting to him!
But no matter.

The crowd prefers
a dive, Bruce swanning
toward the side-

walk in the tortured
pose of a body just
before it becomes

a corpse. So much
for the night's brisk
awakening, the river's

burble, so much
for Bruce Jr.'s sleepy
hair. All that's left

is the idiot mayor
processing down
Fourth Avenue

below the jingoistic
clouds as strips of paper
spiral in the breeze,

hang from branches,
blow in tangled
piles in office doorways,

wrapping Bruce's
body so he can
be born again.

IV
SUPERNOVA

LITTLE EULOGY

Here lies Bruce,
tired out from another
feverish decade.

No priest. No
canny thief. In awe
of the universe

which somehow
unfurled itself
from a tiny

shell. He used to
wander through
the art museum,

startled by the
wide-eyed
horseman's lavish

uniform. Now he
can only stare
at the convulsing

ceiling as the past
blazes up
like a roadside

bomb—the Florida
island where he
and Annie anchored,

their faces bright
as oils. He can still see
a few brushstrokes,

mangroves
twisting thoughtfully
above the water,

the Gulf
going white
in their arms.

SUBVOCAL (SUPERNOVA)

Never be envious of the lonely.
Never long for yr dreary fumbling

twenties driving over oil-soaked
streets for a pocketful

of crappy drugs. Never romanticize
the city, where traffic circles

endlessly, where men
wheel suitcases

of explosives through security.
This robin at the window—

so close you notice
its weird middle toe

dangling over the dark
branch—might be enough.

She quivers nervously.
She's always hungry,

keeping one eye on you,
one on the relentless

future. Never believe the lead singer
is happy. Never rhapsodize

about the Sweet Ole Days
of Mom and Pop.

Never long for someone
else's money. You want

to blow up Bruce? You want yr face
tattooed on a groupie's ass

so when she farts you speak?
Go ahead.

Opine all night.
Opine yr precious lips off.

While time rolls over you
like an Abrams tank.

Pop's got gout. Mom needs
her nap. There's no avoiding

the Future Resident spot
at Brookdale Assisted Living.

You know the joke. Ain't no
brooks or dales where yr going

buddy. Never forget
the world glows

with the energy of 2624 nuclear explosions
plus the sun

there waiting patiently
to swallow us. You can't always be astonished

when it rises red and gold over St. Mary's,
before the merciless horizon

snuffs it out. Know this: yr luck
and the robin's have just about gone

south. Not to worry.
She wants the worm. One light

hop and she's gone.
The branch shudders, then

presses itself back against the sky.
That's all kid. That's it.

TWO BY TWO

Bruce doesn't have much to say
about Annie. He forgets he's lucky.
Forgets she's smarter, works
harder, makes less money.

From other men Bruce learns
to pretend he's worth his salary.
Forgets that lust is only one
blade of their beauty.

And all the days
she holds his melancholy
like a wet, wild animal,
so he can be happy.

BRUCE'S MOOD

is positively mid-
western—a long session
on the couch with no one
listening except the ceiling,
and winter's five-month
hangover around the corner.

This place is all corners, grids
penciled over fields with a grade
school straight edge.
When he was no more
than a thorn, his mother
said he needed structure.

Now look at him. Everyone
else is brunching in Brooklyn,
or putting in the solar
on their cabins. When he stands
to shut the curtain, a cardinal
lands in the lilac

and stares back
with its black suspicious
eye. There are no birds in Brooklyn,
no lilacs in backwoods heaven.
The rising oceans will
take forever to get to him.

The cardinal twitches
on its delicate branch
then flees. Bruce opens
a breezy window.
Orange leaves
pour from the trees.

SUBVOCAL (LIFE SUPPORT)

Hook me up to everything you've got.
Snap electrodes to my temples, pipe

pink froth through my lungs until the blood
runs out. Sew in pig valves, spry and spongy,

a pair of stout bull's balls
if that's the way it has to be.

I'm no good at dying.
I can't stand the thought of missing

a college football season or the latest starlet
crop. I need more time to make things right

with whatever sadist pulled the string
to start me singing.

So keep the fluids coming. Keep a bible on the dresser
just in case. Keep a detailed record

of communiqués blinked out with the one good eye.
And as long as I can tell Beyoncé

from Brittany, beauty
from pornography,

as long as sunlight rattles through the blinds
to shine

on Annie, fierce behind a veil of dust,
you keep that pig heart pumping in my chest.

TRIPLE CROWN

Veined question marks of shrimp,
legs yanked from a chicken, mussels
clattering in the pan after months
of clinging to a sunken rope with what
looks like quiet desperation. The radio plays
the call from the '73 Belmont—Secretariat
moving like a tremendous machine.
Meat, muscle. Cutting through the dark
eyes of a potato. Bruce looks down at his fingers
wrinkling around the knife.
Last night he dreamed he was commander
of a deadly sub and killed a spy
by spraying him with ink from
a poison pen. Every murder begins
with a murderous thought. In between,
we eat. Bruce longs for a defunct era
when we roamed savannas, filthy
and amazed, when a gas burner flaring
to life would have been astonishing—
like a dead bird getting unsteadily to its feet,
shaking its feathers and flying off—
the sort of wondrous sight that led us
to religion. Bruce is skeptical
about the soul, but some evenings
he feels a hunched, bow-legged creature
wallowing in the tar pits of his body,
some mornings it frees itself and bounds
away in the grass, or climbs
haltingly to the top of a broad tree
and looks out across the burning plains
where animals run in frightened circles.

BRUCE IN ORBIT

Red faces float across the rearview mirror.
The snow severe. The radio blahdy
blahdy blahs—mad jihadists
pack nightmares in their Calvin Kleins,
oil blackens the Gulf, the President's
another useless millionaire. Bruce skids
down a slope, tires spinning anxiously
on the ice. He's late. Somewhere summery,
two beautiful actors name their kid
after a minor planet. The President
helicopters into paradise. Bruce's dying
father lies in the hospital again. When he twists
the wheel just right, the car shoots joyously
into traffic. The radio sings. The galaxy takes over.

SUBVOCAL (TICKER)

Ever wonder what they pay
these other fuckers for?

The works-muckers, hall-stalkers, and over-
caffeinated close talkers

with their theories about mercury,
open carry, black ops, black

mold. The power-humpers slipping
memos in the orifices

of upper management
while directives drift

through ductwork like nerve
gas. *Akk! Hachoo!*

You know I'm allergic to that jazz.
Mesh one gear to another, comrade—

that's my philosophy. Stretch yr crisis silk-
thin and hold it up to the latest

supernova, the new
black hole. Remember, Bruce

when you were the most virtuous
bartender in Old Town,

hanging glittery glasses among the lights
while yr barmate fed margaritas

to Jennifer and Jessica or knocked back
Yuenglings with Moby Nick who could talk

all night about his (unfinished) dissertation
on Melville's pentameter.

Ying-ling. Yin and yang. Tashtego.
Mariah Carey. South Philly.

Bon mots disappearing in a haze
of Marlboros. *Like Budweiser, only better.*

It's a flaw Bruce, missing a chance
with the Jersey girls because yr bleary,

sad sack boss might come around
the corner. Here's a little mental exercise:

tally all the drinks you measured perfectly.
Picture every word of yr annual review

carved deeply on yr tombstone.
Click click

go the beads of a cracked abacus.
Tick tick the busted heart

of Jimmy Perth who used to holler
from the roof at high school girls

(something about the stick shift
in his El Camino) while you scraped

lead from ruined Victorians
with a 5-in-1. Soon yr hands

will look like his did then. Soon yr own
daughter will be hooted at by terrible

sad men. Bleep bleep Bruce. Bleep bleep
the cornflakes in the scanner beam.

Bleep bleep the birds,
the 6:00 a.m. alarm. Bleep bleep

the words you think but never say.
Wake up! It's garbage day—time

to roll out last week's leavings
as dawn wheezes through the fog

and a gasping truck lifts two blue toters
with its awful claw.

Down yr coffee. Holler up the stairs.
Come on kids. Shake a feather.

It's time to bleep!
Time to get to work.

ACKNOWLEDGMENTS

I would like to thank the editors of the following journals, in which some of these poems first appeared:

Birmingham Poetry Review: "Bruce's Mood"
Borderlands: Texas Poetry Review: "Museum of Natural History"
Chattahoochee Review: "Reality TV"
Copper Nickel: "Curriculum"
Diagram: "Subvocal (Counterterror)"
Faultline: "Subvocal (Honky)"
Escape Into Life: "Unborn Elegy"
FIELD: "The Economy Stupid" and "Intelligent Design"
Florida Review: "Little Eulogy"
Gulf Coast: "Subvocal (Hadley)"
Hunger Mountain: "Drone View," "Subvocal (Supermodel)," and "Oof"
Louisville Review: "Homunculus" and "Two Dimensions"
Rhino: "Totem"
New England Review: "Triple Crown," "Automaton," and "Bruce's Faith"
Passages North: "Star Vehicle"
Slice Magazine: "Subvocal (Challenger)"
Southern Indiana Review: "First Blood" and "United Church of Bruce"
Willow Springs: "Subvocal (Jefferson Airplane)"

I am grateful to the National Endowment for the Arts and Ball State University for their generous support.

Thank you Alia Bales, Brian Barker, Rick Barot, Nicky Beer, Taylor Bratches, Ken Hart, Tom Haushalter, John Hoppenthaler, Justin Janisse, Kathleen Kirk, Samantha Kolber, Robin McCarthy, Wayne Miller, Ron Mitchell, Ander Monson, Adam Vines, David Walker, Marcus Wicker, Ted Worozbyt, and David Young for their generous support of my work.

Thank you Jackson Holbert, Christine Holbert, and Lost Horse Press for believing in this book, and taking such care to bring it to life. And thank you Christopher Howell for the conversation and sage advice.

Enormous gratitude to all my teachers, even all these years later. And to Bob Hicok and Teun Hocks for your kindness, and your startling, radiant work.

Thanks Ander and Sean and the Order of the Jags. Ring the chains.

Thanks Tim Earley for the dog videos and the rtr.

Thank you to my brilliant and generous friends and colleagues, especially Tim Berg, Cindy Collier, Pat Collier, Katy Didden, Jackie Grutsch McKinney, Todd McKinney, and Debbie Mix.

Endless love and gratitude to Mom, Juliet, and Sophia. And Martha Christman.

In memory of Wright Neely and Pete Christman. Rest in peace.

Thank you Jill, Ella, and Henry for all our adventures, large and small.